50 THINGS TO KNOW BOOK SERIES REVIEWS FROM READERS

I recently downloaded a couple of books from this series to read over the weekend thinking I would read just one or two. However, I so loved the books that I read all the six books I had downloaded in one go and ended up downloading a few more today. Written by different authors, the books offer practical advice on how you can perform or achieve certain goals in life, which in this case is how to have a better life.

The information is simple to digest and learn from, and is incredibly useful. There are also resources listed at the end of the book that you can use to get more information.

50 Things To Know To Have A Better Life: Self-Improvement Made Easy!

Author Dannii Cohen

This book is very helpful and provides simple tips on how to improve your everyday life. I found it to be useful in improving my overall attitude.

50 Things to Know For Your Mindfulness & Meditation Journey
Author Nina Edmondso

Quick read with 50 short and easy tips for what to think about before starting to homeschool.

50 Things to Know About Getting Started with Homeschool by Author Amanda Walton

I really enjoyed the voice of the narrator, she speaks in a soothing tone. The book is a really great reminder of things we might have known we could do during stressful times, but forgot over the years.

Author Harmony Hawaii

There is so much waste in our society today. Everyone should be forced to read this book. I know I am passing it on to my family.

50 Things to Know to Downsize Your Life: How To Downsize, Organize, And Get Back to Basics

Author Lisa Rusczyk Ed. D.

Great book to get you motivated and understand why you may be losing motivation. Great for that person who wants to start getting healthy, or just for you when you need motivation while having an established workout routine.

50 Things To Know To Stick With A Workout: Motivational Tips To Start The New You Today

Author Sarah Hughes

50 THINGS TO KNOW ABOUT HAVING A WORK-LIFE BALANCE

Working From Home Tips & Tricks

Brandy Pan

50 Things to Know About Having a Work-Life Balance
Copyright © 2021 by CZYK Publishing LLC.
All Rights Reserved.

All rights reserved. No part of this book may be reproduced in any form or by any electronic or mechanical means including information storage and retrieval systems, without permission in writing from the author. The only exception is by a reviewer, who may quote short excerpts in a review.

The statements in this book are of the authors and may not be the views of CZYK Publishing or 50 Things to Know.

Cover designed by: Ivana Stamenkovic
Cover Image: https://pixabay.com/photos/wfh-work-from-home-covid19-5010034/

CZYK Publishing Since 2011.
CZYKPublishing.com
50 Things to Know

Lock Haven, PA
All rights reserved.
ISBN: 9798748600026

50 Things to Know

50 THINGS TO KNOW ABOUT HAVING A WORK-LIFE BALANCE

BOOK DESCRIPTION

How do I optimize my days so I live a fulfilled life without regrets? What choices can I make to have a better life balance when I juggle my busy life and work from home? How can I reset and restore balance when I feel off? If you're not sure of the answers to any of these questions, then this book is for you...

50 Things to Know About Having a Work-Life Balance by Author Brandy Pan offers an approach to optimize your life in a growing virtual world. Most books on work-life balance address how to be successful in our lives before our world changed drastically in 2020. Although there's nothing wrong with that, work-from-home life has become the new way to make work for you.

Based on knowledge from the world's leading experts, pivoting to a new normal has changed everything from the way we work to our mental health, how we shop, and the ways we socialize. To stay relevant and connected, we're balancing and co-adapting virtual life into our real life.

In these pages you'll discover new perspectives and reminders on how to navigate a balanced life in our advanced world and prepare us for the next technological growth… This book will help you consider what's working and guide you to think about changes you want to make. Balance is like a food that's fragrant and tasty, and medicine to our mind-bodies. Finding the delicate balance for your life is going to leave you feeling satisfied.

By the time you finish this book, you will know if you're headed in the right direction for a whole, and successful life, and for this season…. So grab YOUR copy today. You'll be glad you did.

TABLE OF CONTENTS

50 Things to Know
Book Series
Reviews from Readers
BOOK DESCRIPTION
TABLE OF CONTENTS
DEDICATION
ABOUT THE AUTHOR
INTRODUCTION
1. Create Designated Spaces For Work, Personal, And Social/Family Activities
2. Take Personal Time And Days Off
3. Check-in Regularly To See If You're Headed On The Right Path For Your Satisfying Life
4. Make And Revisit A List Of Aspirations And Dreams
5. Check Your Emotional Temperature
6. Check Your Daily Diet
7. Maintain A 5-minute Per Day Exercise Habit For Your Health and Energy
8. Find Weekly Quiet-time For Reflection Or Meditation
9. You Get To Decide What's Most Important To You As You Can Have It All, But Maybe Not All At The Same Time

10. Own What Success Means To You
11. Say No To Ideas That Are Not Good For You
12. Planning Out Your Meals Will Help You Find Life Balance
13. Decorating, lighting, and using color splashes in your spaces can inspire you
14. If You Have Corporate Hours, Pace Yourself
15. Find Ways To Join Work Groups And Collaborate With Others
16. Preserve Your Most Productive "Golden Hours"
17. Take 10-minute Breaks For Every Hour Of Work
18. If You Have Long Commute Times, Use The Time Wisely To Audibly Learn A New Language or New Song
19. Create Time Management Boundaries With Others
20. Set Aside Time To Straighten Up Your Areas
21. Set Personal Time Rules That You Hold Sacred
22. Reward Yourself When You Complete Milestones And Goals
23. Use Tools That You Can Share With A Push Of A Button
24. Keep Your Watching News And Television Time Down To A Minimum
25. Measure Your Virtual Time On Devices And Ensure You Have A Balance With Real Life

26. Ask For What You Need
27. Reset Your Feelings and Moods
28. Find New Ways To Add "-ive" Descriptors To Your Life
29. Build Systems In Your Work And Life
30. Define Your Work Purpose
31. Set Out To Find Your Life Purpose
32. Keep A Consistent Personality
33. Keep A List Of 3-4 Things You Want To Accomplish Each Day
34. Use Mundane Chores As Time To Be Mindful And Present
35. Always Think Overnight Before Committing
36. Keep Moving In A Forward, Growing Up Direction
37. Find Daily Inspiration
38. Have No Judgment
39. Batch Work Days
40. Allow Space For You To Grow Into
41. Hire Help For Tasks You Don't Enjoy Or Where It Makes Sense
42. Reset To Loving Thoughts And Find Love In Life's Beauty
43. Find Time To Dream About This Life
44. Laugh And Have Fun

45. Find Like-minded Networks And Groups To Interact With.
46. Stay Grounded. When You Can Stay Humble and Peace-filled, Then You Be Incredibly Useful To Others
47. Flip Any Negative Perspective Around
48. Find A Creative Activity That Uses A Side Of Your Brain That You Don't Use In Your Work Or Daily
49. Find A Way To Spread More Loving-kindness To Your Day
50. Mind-body balance

Other Helpful Resources

50 Things to Know

DEDICATION

This book is dedicated to those who have lost loved ones or experienced job loss from the 2020 pandemic.

ABOUT THE AUTHOR

Brandy Pan is the author of Empowered Happiness. After several life pivots from a corporate working life, she took a mid-life sabbatical, that re directed her to find a balanced, healthy path for success.

She is currently a freelance writer, blogger, and mentor. You can learn how to restore your mind-body balance and get healthy tips weekly at https://healthyhappylifesecrets.com

INTRODUCTION

"Life is like a bicycle. To keep your balance you must keep moving."

-Albert Einstein

Albert Einstein is remembered for his brains and scientific theories, but he also gave us the beginning notes to support our modern mind-body connection awareness.

As little as 30 minutes a day of mindful new normal activities, and purposeful habit changes can provide the optimal work-life balance you want.

1. CREATE DESIGNATED SPACES FOR WORK, PERSONAL, AND SOCIAL/FAMILY ACTIVITIES

Creating zones can provide order and peace of mind that can be more important for mental health than larger accomplishments.

You may want to shut the door of your designated office space, or your computer when you're done with work for the day. Change your clothing and socks like you would if you went to work and came home.

Having a ritual will keep you from burning out when you have one home base for work, life, and home.

Consider the outside and your outdoor space as a place for you to catch a break and get new insight.

Taking several hour walks and mindful breaks away from where you spend 80% or more of your day and sleeping hours can be healthy to daily restore you.

2. TAKE PERSONAL TIME AND DAYS OFF

This will make your work worthwhile and give you a chance to rest. Our bodies need more rest than we think or give ourselves.

That's important for you to take time off even if you feel like you're on vacation or working from home.

Mind rest is needed and is good for long-term health. If you live in America, that's not the norm. Vacation days can be few if you don't make them a priority. Many Americans take their work with them on vacation.

Recuperating from daily grind keeps you from work-life burnout.

Try not to work on the weekends or at least one day of the week. If you add up the number of those days, that's almost two months. If you consider taking off those two months plus additional vacation time or as much as you can. Your body can reward you in your marathon long run.

Stress is rampant and the silent killer. One day there's a stress gray hair or a stress pimple. The next day that becomes an inflammation. And one day your body can just break.

Use "you will not get this time" back as your guide and reasoning motivator to find time to relax.

Italians know the sweetness of doing nothing (dolce far niente) and Croatians have the same 'relax' (fjaka) philosophies of life that American society can learn from for better life balance.

3. CHECK-IN REGULARLY TO SEE IF YOU'RE HEADED ON THE RIGHT PATH FOR YOUR SATISFYING LIFE

This way you don't wake up with regrets. Use your open-minded intuition and higher intellect conscience to guide you.

Use all the signs from your emotions to reflect inwardly. If you haven't been working from home, you can forget to do this in the busyness or around others.

We can get so busy we miss the weigh-in points. If you don't see a light-at-the-end-of-tunnel, that can mean there's a better solution.

It could mean you could give more love to other areas of your life or get a new perspective on the one that's not ideal.

Being honest with yourself is the most satisfying decision you can make.

Some workplaces start off good, but can take a turn. Sustainability vs. burnout can be a reason for staying put. If the future looks promising then the day-to-day changes can be more manageable.

Many unhappy workers can see that their work is providing them less anxiety than if they were not working.

Plus they have a greater motivational reason to seek something else from their current unhappiness.

4. MAKE AND REVISIT A LIST OF ASPIRATIONS AND DREAMS

If you have dreamt an idea before, that can become a possibility in your better timing now or in the future.

For this year think about what you really think you want and can accomplish. Planning for the next 2 years is more realistic than having your entire life planned out for retirement.

For the next 5 years, think of a few goals you want to achieve and daydream about those and how you can carry those out, maybe sooner.

No matter what you plan, your plans will change and can turn out better.

The silver lining to change is that you will not be bored. You will learn more things as once you get in the groove of a job, you can start to relax as the learning curve isn't as steep.

When you have a chance to catch your breath, you can think about your life aspirations.

For your dream bucket list from now to the end of your life, list out everything you want to have experienced and acheived.

Then take a look at this list and see if anything jumps out at you that maybe you want to move up in time. When you find these previously hidden desires, then you can change the way you prioritize your life. You can discover what's on your heart becomes more important.

If your desire is to visit a place you've never been to, or do something you've never done, that's going to exert time and energy in another direction.

So that may require you to make critical decisions for your deepest desires to happen sooner.

Or you will find a way to balance your work-life better.

5. CHECK YOUR EMOTIONAL TEMPERATURE

Feelings act as the compass that guides us daily and the decisions we make. Love, passion, and compassion help you navigate.

Are you feeling irritated or anxious? If you are triggered, you can be taking out your feelings on others.

Under pressure, below the surface feelings can surface. They're not as obvious as laughter and tears, and unless you make a point to observe them or your associated behaviors, you may not get awareness.

Without acknowledgement, you could be carrying unhappy burdens. The only people who don't want to be around happy people are unhappy people. Misery loves company.

You're better to stay happy and let your optimistic ways overflow. Staying emotionally consistent or even keel, instead of reacting to swinging highs and lows will help you feel balanced and in control.

6. CHECK YOUR DAILY DIET

It's easy to get off-course and pick up bad habits we didn't mean to adopt, and then that becomes our life until we decide to change course.

The foods you consume play a large role in your feeling balanced as most of the happy hormones are created in the gut.

If you eat a less nutritious meal, then that can change your mood or concentration. If you eat a heavier lunch, that can slow you down in productivity in the afternoon.

If you don't eat enough, then your stomach can start growling and you may be moody, feel dizzy, or have low blood sugar.

If you have signs of a change in your physical health, take notice of the foods you eat. You hear too many scenarios where people play down their symptoms so they don't have to be reminded and that becomes their norm. Your body sends warnings for a reason.

Preventative health and food as medicine is not a focus area in America. If you take care of your well-being now, you can have infinite, optimum physical and mental health in your finite years.

If you keep a healthy pantry, you won't go hungry and won't as likely reach for an unhealthy snack.

7. MAINTAIN A 5-MINUTE PER DAY EXERCISE HABIT FOR YOUR HEALTH AND ENERGY

You will feel better if you get your exercise in. That's why we have gadgets to measure our progress, steps, and exercise.

If you include exercising daily in your routine, you're more likely to maintain your habit, and then you can increase to an hour or more per week. You'll be glad you did that day and when you're older. Working out can help with your energy and success. A few ideas:

Having a mat rolled out and ready to go can be a good visual reminder.

Find compatible exercises and ways to stay accountable.

From anywhere and during breaks, you can always do push ups, situps, and side-bends, and they count.

Doing jumping jacks where you are is a good way to get your cardio in, heartbeat up, and pump energy into you if you feel tired.

If you sit in front of a computer all day, having tight arms, neck and shoulders are common. So shaking it all out and looking up will help your neck and shoulders. Stretch your arms and up above your head to give your shoulders a rest.

When you have a little more time and if you're low in energy, doing some standing or floor stretches can change the way you feel.

You may find fitness videos are good to add back to your practice. They can be 10 minutes or longer and before you know it, you've done more than 5 minutes per day.

Changing your groove and having exercise variety can sometimes get you enthusiastic about exercise again.

8. FIND WEEKLY QUIET-TIME FOR REFLECTION OR MEDITATION

This is the much-needed peace we need. Find what your heart is telling you.

Select a day where you don't have back-to-back appointments. Let your beating heart settle down.

Getting calm helps to optimize this quiet time, that doesn't have to be more than 30 minutes of quality time to have impact.

If you have lingering negative thoughts, distraction is a good first step. That's why journaling or scribbling out your thoughts on paper you can shred, works. You can use this designated time of the week to write out your gratitude thoughts in a journal.

When you do this, your mind switches to a place of contentment, similar to how you feel when you're receiving vs. giving.

While receiving in gratitude, it's easier to be content.

If you find that you keep getting a whispered answer like "now what?" then you may want to lean in and try to see what comes back in thoughts.

Let go of any unproductive thoughts and think of growth.

You could encourage growth thoughts with a simple endeavor such as caring for a plant you take care of or a daily activity you do that is enjoyable and effortless given your skills, talents, and abilities.

9. YOU GET TO DECIDE WHAT'S MOST IMPORTANT TO YOU AS YOU CAN HAVE IT ALL, BUT MAYBE NOT ALL AT THE SAME TIME

Pick, prioritize, and decide. Otherwise, you can be overwhelmed or disappointed you didn't give your all to an area of your life.

Don't bite off more than you can chew.

You don't want a bunch of projects you didn't accomplish or doing activities half-heartedly because you stated you would.

Instead of stating aloud (or declaring to others) in advance what you will do in action and then possibly having inaction occur, consider the idea first and then move forward.

Life's a marathon, not a sprint.

As you get older, you feel this more. You linger on the moments more as you go through life's seasons. The last season may never show up again (and that can be good).

The value in tough situations is that you know what you don't want again. You've been there, done that. And you learn better ways for you now to navigate. Life is about experiencing and growing, and that's why you don't become a child again.

It's easy to bury the past that can help you to navigate a better future. Look at each part of life as a reason or a season. Some seasons can last longer and others shorter. Not putting a length of time on a season can be freeing. Length of time doesn't determine your happiness, you do.

What can seem like a good idea at the time or a shiny object, may add stress to your life as another uncompleted activity. You'll know when you can take on more because you'll be asking what now? That's when you know you need more than what is available to you.

A good example of this is with social media platforms. Stick to one or two in the beginning and participate. If you find that there are reasons to join others, then consider the idea and test the waters. Try this with your other small, low-risk activities in your life and then apply them to the larger things.

When you're at home, you have less travel time.

You can focus more on prioritizing what's important. You can also get inside your head more than you would, so be sure to keep balanced with getting outside into the local community.

10. OWN WHAT SUCCESS MEANS TO YOU

Everyone agrees they want to be happy, but what makes happiness is a different set of ideas for each person.

You can lower the bar and that can get you further as you take any Impostor Syndrome or self-doubt out of the way.

Often we adopt someone else's idea of what success means and we don't know all the specifics. Then we can be disappointed in our outcome. A better approach is if you think about how that strategy can work for you in tactics and with your personality.

A good question to ask yourself is, "if you didn't have to worry about your life, what would you do differently?" Then put the possibility back in your world. Because if you can dream, it's not impossible. Use your heart to guide you in deeper desires as there's a unique destiny for you.

And if you find someone has done something similar, you can build on that proof to create your success.

11. SAY NO TO IDEAS THAT ARE NOT GOOD FOR YOU

You do everyone a favor so that you can focus on what your true calling is.

By saying no you've allowed for other possibilities to enter.

If you start this habit, you will notice that you are happier. If you feel guilt, that our brains are wired to do, then you can remove that by reasoning that what's right for someone else, doesn't mean it's right for you.

So someone who creates a new scenario for you is asking you to participate in their causes. If you can do so with a loving heart, but you will resent signing up for the cause later on or the person who asked you, don't.

They would prefer you didn't either in the long run despite their immediate excitement. You can always say, I need to think/pray about it (depending on which you would do).

If in your heart or gut you know that you should decline, then do so kindly and give them a short honest reason that's about you and your situation (not about them and their cause or situation).

For example, you mention you don't think you're the right person because… or you mention you're overwhelmed these days… this keeps peaceful thoughts so you can move on from this ask, and they can also. If you hem and haw, they can still try to convince you, so be sure you know your stance on what you're willing and able to do before you reply. They will respect you and you will feel empowered.

12. PLANNING OUT YOUR MEALS WILL HELP YOU FIND LIFE BALANCE

You'll get more time back and have better, quality meals with thoughtful and healthier ingredients if you choose.

By prepping meals and food, taking time to create meals is healthier and also allows you to take time to focus on tasks and digest better by slower chewing. You also have food ready if you get hungry-angry (hangry) and moody when you don't have food.

You'd be surprised how much time making individual meals can make. That all adds up and we all have the same amount of time.

If you prepare your meals then you can control the ingredient intake and your healthy eating habits better. You can balance healthy eating over consuming your less healthy favorites in moderation as what goes in joyfully affects your physical and mental health.

13. DECORATING, LIGHTING, AND USING COLOR SPLASHES IN YOUR SPACES CAN INSPIRE YOU

Shades of color can make a difference in your daily happiness.

On paint strips, analogous colors can go from light to dark and those gradual shade changes can be the difference between white to gray that are both neutrals. Even neutrals convey different feelings with their undertones.

Gray can be soothing to the eyes, while stark-white can convey a minimalist or perfectionist color. We all have our favorites and different technicolor coming from our eyes and monitors.

Colors can attract or they can repel. That's why male birds are shockingly bright-colored to attract females. There's a visceral response that our eyes communicate to impact the happy parts of our minds.

When you see a warm color like yellow, you can't help but feel energetic and happy, which can inspire you. When you see more subtle colors like pastels, they are calming.

When you play around with colors in your life, they can create a better mood.

Use them in your virtual world on screensavers and backgrounds, to inspire and make your 2-D world come alive.

14. IF YOU HAVE CORPORATE HOURS, PACE YOURSELF

We often see our lives as either gaining or else losing time, money, or energy that can be more important to conserve.

When you have to work certain hours, when you can get a free moment, take a mindful moment and look outside or rest your eyes from the computer.

It's easy to keep working and that can tire and burn you out faster than if you took the slow-and-steady-wins-the-race approach.

Think of yourself as a business owner and not as an employee. Find ways to be strategic and do the important tasks. When you don't think like someone who doesn't clock in and out, then you can get out of seeing yourself as an hourly worker who is limited in output.

Set artificial timers to have a stopping point. If you're not on a deadline, the work will still be there tomorrow when you have a fresh perspective.

15. FIND WAYS TO JOIN WORK GROUPS AND COLLABORATE WITH OTHERS

When you co-mingle you have influence, can make deeper impact, and create lasting relationships.

When you join a workgroup, you know you have at least one thing in common -- the same employer. So naturally, you want to discuss other topics because you breathe the same air. This can be helpful to learn about others outside of your work bubble, so you can appreciate your work for more than just a building with walls where you take care of business-work.

When you can learn about your co-workers then you can break down the walls that separate you and them. You see them as humans just like you. Then when you're in the same meetings and conversations, you understand their perspective from other angles. And even if you do disagree, you find it's okay to agree to disagree because at the end of the day we can talk again on lighter subjects.

These days people are more open about themselves at work so you're not as likely to see the professional vs. personal demeanor of a person that doesn't match up.

Find new groups to join in social media. You sometimes have to go outside your immediate circle to find what you're looking for. If you were looking for a tennis partner, you'd want to check tennis groups and people who play at the same level as you. The circles become smaller once you start researching.

16. PRESERVE YOUR MOST PRODUCTIVE "GOLDEN HOURS"

We all have better times of the day to do certain tasks where we're on fire and moving efficiently as our brains cooperate.

If we need to be creative, that can be strong in the morning when our brain is fresh and clear. By afternoon, we are naturally more tired and some of us catch a second wind.

You also want to do as much as possible early in the morning in case something throws you off the rest of the day. So then you at least got something worthwhile done.

Prioritize the activity that will move the needle for you the most. Get that mountain task out of the way. Morning could be a good time to get in cardio exercising.

When you break up your day by the number of activities accomplished over actual time, then that can work to your advantage as you feel you've done more versus losing time that slips by.

17. TAKE 10-MINUTE BREAKS FOR EVERY HOUR OF WORK

You'll be able to focus better if you know there's a break in sight.

We all need refreshing moments and 10 minutes is long enough to do some invigorating jumping jacks, step outside, read a few words of inspiration, look out your window or make a snack.

These quick breaks can refresh your mind, energy level, and prepare you for the next hour ahead along with the remaining hours of the day. When we're immersed in what we're doing we can miss out on the valuable, ordinary moments.

We've all learned that life is fragile as we've seen so much happening, and that has made moments more precious.

Work less and produce more. More time doesn't mean better work. You can lose sight of what is quality work while going through the motions.

If you're a business owner, you know that working on your business can be more effective than working in your business.

You need both, but you can outsource many tasks and tactics, so you can focus on the activities that matter.

18. IF YOU HAVE LONG COMMUTE TIMES, USE THE TIME WISELY TO AUDIBLY LEARN A NEW LANGUAGE OR NEW SONG

Listening to an audio podcast or radio message can keep you grounded, growing, and inspired -- keeping what's happening in your life in perspective.

Then you can continue the learning when you find downtime. You can learn a new language by adding subtitles to your watching screen or improve your health.

You can smooth out rougher moments getting to and from by stimulating your mind. Listening to happy music can also put you in a good mood.

If you're not traveling while working from home, take that same time and learn a new skill. Not having to travel, you can increase your learning.

Whether you're stuck in traffic or not driving, take moments to appreciate where you are observing changes in nature outside and using those changes as metaphor comparisons for where you are in life.

This could be learning new words and replacing ways we say things. This can sound like sugarcoating words except we are better off being purposeful with our words instead of letting our minds do the talking.

19. CREATE TIME MANAGEMENT BOUNDARIES WITH OTHERS

When you work from home and are more accessible to house members, set boundaries and be consistent. Encourage others to book their time with you so there are fewer interruptions during your golden hours.

By using a calendar, for work appointments, you can prepare for your appointment. For friend meetups, you can plan and look forward to the next time you can catch up.

By your actions, show people in your life what your hours are and for what activities.

When you say "yes" to an activity or change your activity, you are training others involved in what is acceptable to you. Besides, you could end up resenting others.

Create boundaries based on what's best for the long term. Then stick with them consistently.

Preserve your time. There's enough to do when you're in charge of your schedule, to not have others control your time even if it's just for half an hour.

You could have used that time to catch up with all your email or read an article that gives you an idea that becomes your new strategy.

20. SET ASIDE TIME TO STRAIGHTEN UP YOUR AREAS

When your spaces are in disarray, the clutter can permeate into our minds and make us feel like we're not in control.

This sets our rhythm off. We can take longer to make decisions with our minds in distraction.

If we stop to take time to get things in order then we can feel like a weight is lifted off of us and we feel productive. Depending on you and your personality, this can allow you to feel free to pursue other thoughts and activities.

Dusting can seem like an afterthought, but when you realize how much shinier your home looks, you can feel rewarded, dusting more often and feeling better.

21. SET PERSONAL TIME RULES THAT YOU HOLD SACRED

If you are not working or are taking a vacation, if you have to check in with others, set expectations when you will be available.

Find moments to disconnect and be "off the grid" unless there's an emergency.

The more often you don't respond, helps your brain realize that you don't need to act. You can feel invisible freedom that builds into your life satisfaction.

We all have self-care nuances in our lives that we need to take care of. Everyone, including extroverts or young dependents need personal time.

22. REWARD YOURSELF WHEN YOU COMPLETE MILESTONES AND GOALS

Take the afternoon off to recharge or celebrate when you've completed a big goal.

Life wouldn't be worth living if we couldn't enjoy bits and pieces in our milestones and victories and then share them with others.

You can find joy in simple things like visiting your favorite spots and parks. Nature is an outdoor exhibition that runs 24-7. Fun is what you make out of the moment.

Have some fun and then get back to reality as soon as possible, as you want to keep the productive momentum going. When you're on a streak, you want to keep moving along.

23. USE TOOLS THAT YOU CAN SHARE WITH A PUSH OF A BUTTON

Automation saves us time and energy and we can find all kinds of ways to balance our lives out. If you need productivity tools, there are so many to choose from.

There are many project management tools available. You can learn simple tips and tricks by doing quick searches.

Learning how to use the features of the tools the way they are intended can save you productive time and energy.

We forget to label, archive, and micro-organize our email inboxes daily. Then that slows us down as we can't find what we need to focus on in a reasonable amount of time.

24. KEEP YOUR WATCHING NEWS AND TELEVISION TIME DOWN TO A MINIMUM

When you let the television run from one show to the next, that's when you want to be mindfully careful.

Your mind can easily drift to the negative places that encourage fear-based thinking tendencies.

To catch up enough, 30-60 minutes per day of watching or reading the news will provide an adequate update for the day.

By recording your favorite shows and watching them later when you need a break, you can achieve more and feel less anxious, like you missed out (fear of missing out is a common feeling that enters at some point in our lives). We can change this if we know how to flip our perspectives.

When you embrace positive change, you learn to "let go." That's your ticket to freedom, happiness, and peace. Life is meant to have setbacks, twists, and turns so you can grow.

If you fight the tide or go against the grain of the wood, then that makes your journey more difficult. When you go with the flow, then you can focus on finding the best ways to use your situations.

25. MEASURE YOUR VIRTUAL TIME ON DEVICES AND ENSURE YOU HAVE A BALANCE WITH REAL LIFE

If you work on a computer all day, have time where you are communicating with people in other ways. Keep track of how many hours you have electronics running or are on digital devices.

Virtual reality has become a society reality.

The best mix is to have both so you get a 360-degree life, 365 days of the year. We want to live pre-2000 when the internet was only a few years old. Those times aren't coming back. But we also don't want to be like robots in an AI age.

Set up your own boundaries and how often you'll check in with social media. Select which ones you will be active on and which you will be passive on.

You may want to meet new friends other than the ones you grew up with, went to school with, or worked with.

The blend can be intentional and if you're part of the virtual-reality world, that's a hybrid between being on Zoom and being in the room. Our phones are being used less for phone calls and more for texting and watching videos.

26. ASK FOR WHAT YOU NEED

If you ask specific and kindly what you want someone to do for you, they are more likely to do it than if you leave as a suggestion for them.

Give simple instructions and allow for outcomes other than what you hope for. Then you're more likely to be pleasantly surprised and not disappointed.

If you expect a quick response, you may be putting energy into the wrong thoughts that consume you. When you forget about it, that's when the results can show up.

Believe that your inner desires will happen (with or without people), and not necessarily in the way you may think. When the good things manifest, all that didn't feel right at the time will be made right.

27. RESET YOUR FEELINGS AND MOODS

Thoughts in the mind impact your body, and your body impacts your mind (mind-body connection).

If you're feeling stress, you start to get worried, anxious, critical, and those feelings can show up as inflammations. That's the body's way of communicating change is needed. Chronic or acute stress can be an indicator that something needs to change.

You also want to prevent negative emotions or moods from lingering as they show up in the body, usually in a delayed fashion.

Moods that linger for a season are trying to tell you something.

You may not know what that is until you take a leap in faith. Meaning comes out on the other, better side.

Lean into your body's natural desires as they indicate what you may need more of, such as flavoring spices can help to show you what your body needs. The same spices can be favorable or repulsive to your sense of smell in different seasons of your life.

Lean into your healthy, natural thoughts. Be discerning and reject your negative or ego-based thoughts. If you want to improve your life, observe your thoughts like a third-party witness and listener. You don't have to act on your thoughts or even continue with your thoughts that don't need a response.

Distract your unloving thoughts by doing simple tasks. Being appreciative of changing your socks or moisturizing your hands can make you feel better and help change your thoughts to gratitude.

28. FIND NEW WAYS TO ADD "-IVE" DESCRIPTORS TO YOUR LIFE

Innovative, productive, or creative are all high-seeking description words to bring more to the world. Many descriptive words end in "-ive" including "active," "positive," and "sensitive."

The best "-ive" word is "live." The choice is yours to live abundantly or with a limited mindset.

The reminding thoughts of the past can be used to propel you to a better life. You know what it's like to live "less-than" and now is your time to claim a life of victory and full.

Make your life work for you.

29. BUILD SYSTEMS IN YOUR WORK AND LIFE

If you find backup support or systems, you will get more time.

The tradeoff with a busy life is that there's less free time. With strategy and processes, you gain time back.

You gain efficiency and when you want to measure or gauge if your work is working then systemizing will help you do that.

It's easier to create your systems up front, and change them as needed so you don't have to start from scratch when you're in the weeds. If you don't know, just guess what you need and pivot from the new and changing standing point. That way you have something to grow on.

You may have to find your deeper WHY you're doing something. Because when you say yes to one pursuit, you're saying no to another.

This is an opportunity cost that can be more costly than losing money or time. You may or may not know all the opportunities lost until you have free time again.

30. DEFINE YOUR WORK PURPOSE

Your work may have a defined vision or mission, but have you decided what your specific mission or assignment is? Because when you do, then you will own your time.

Pivoting and re-invention is something that you may have gotten good with. You can be adaptable, versatile, and flexible that are beneficial traits for thriving.

You may not have discovered that in every work assignment, but each one has or had a purpose. You could add volunteer, a hobby passion, or a side hustle to your list of activities for accelerated growth.

Pursuing businesses as creative outlets and passions is common for those who want to have a starting side business in our evolving gig economy.

These occurrences are becoming more frequent as the evolving digital and global economy has created obtainable and affordable ways for those who are willing to contribute using their abilities, gifts, talents, skills, creativity, effort, time, and energy.

31. SET OUT TO FIND YOUR LIFE PURPOSE

Every day you have the opportunity to wake up and start a new day in your perspective. See each day as a new possibility to make an impact with your heart's desires.

Anything can happen and a new spark can be ignited. The timing could be right where you reach the tipping point.

Suddenly you can get a new perspective or revelation that can start out as a small-seed idea. When you're intentional in finding your work purpose, you can also find clues to your life purpose. By taking action, you gain clarity and eliminate what you don't want.

Your purpose can be completely different than your work. Use your intuition and heart as internal guides. Your purpose could be a person, group of people, a mission, an activity, or all.

You always have at least one purpose that can change. They will lead you to your destiny that can look completely different than when you started. A caterpillar's main purpose is to become a butterfly, and a butterfly is a beauty to the garden and people. They also help fruits, vegetables, and flowers create new seeds.

32. KEEP A CONSISTENT PERSONALITY

When I started working, it was common to have two personas, one that was personal away from work and another professional while being "on." Those worlds are blending into your one personality or brand.

These were pre-social media days. As part of the evolving social media zeitgeist, authenticity is valued. Nowadays you can show up more like yourself and less like you're "on" in every situation.

In the beginning, employers would try to see what their future employees were like on their "off-time" through social media. Now, work-life is blended and employees have gotten smarter not posting what they don't want to show.

The concept of vulnerability has replaced weakness. Collaboration over competition so your protective guard can come down.

33. KEEP A LIST OF 3-4 THINGS YOU WANT TO ACCOMPLISH EACH DAY

Avoid multitasking, as you get less effectively done, half-listening and doing, and ending up more overwhelmed.

When you cross off your list or keep a list, you stay focused and on task. Keep rewriting and prioritizing your list.

When you see your familiar handwriting over impersonal typed words, that can be more meaningful.

When you focus on what you did do versus what didn't get done, you feel better and that builds your self-esteem.

34. USE MUNDANE CHORES AS TIME TO BE MINDFUL AND PRESENT

Your chores will go by faster. And you can enjoy the thoughtful moments. When you fold clothes or put away dishes, you can allow good ideas to enter, that can be put to use same day or in the future.

Old dreams you put away have a chance to resurrect. Those ideas can lead to your next life-giving endeavor.

Seemingly boring moments can be built up to sweep you into a season of exciting and adventurous swerves.

35. ALWAYS THINK OVERNIGHT BEFORE COMMITTING

When you sleep on an idea, you'd be surprised at how different you can feel or think the next day.

The next day, a reply or decision needed doesn't feel so urgent as more time passes.

The idea may have lost its wings. Yesterday's excitement is replaced with a fresh canvas to paint new ideas.

No longer an emergency, you gain clarity.

36. KEEP MOVING IN A FORWARD, GROWING UP DIRECTION

Whatever path you choose, the right one is moving forward. Don't go backward as a safety net. Keep plowing forward. Life is meant to move you on and up.

That makes making decisions easier. You don't have to wonder if your past decisions were better. They were in the past.

We're always given new sets of circumstances as our external world is revolving, and you're evolving making decisions based on more than what you did in the past.

Life is meant to get better as you age. Keep that as a compass guide like the three wise men who followed the stars.

37. FIND DAILY INSPIRATION

Make a point to find daily ways to ignite a spark in you. If you put away a treasured object, you can rediscover new and interesting facets to the piece.

When you do this with your work or life that has become boring or routine, you can rediscover parts of you and your amazing life that you took for granted.

Inspiration can come from uplifting media, nature, collaboration efforts, researching, curiosity, or a question someone has that you can answer.

The observant and resourceful you become, the more inspiration you can find.

38. HAVE NO JUDGMENT

When you let go of perfectionism, having to be right, judging others, or the outcome, then you have a chance to find peace every day and allow new ideas to grow or flow through you.

If someone offends you, not judging their action is how you gain back your day. Stick with the facts.

You don't want to put energy towards something that happened hours ago (past) and no longer affects you, that you're now spending more time complaining over. Let go of the sour moods by distracting your moment.

If you let the thoughts fade, then you can have your peace back. Imagine letting go of a balloon and watching it soar into the sky never to be seen again.

Everything isn't so easy to release. Having opinions can be helpful to make decisions, if they are peaceful and don't have attached negative emotions. Conversely, judgment comes from a place of fear or insecurity, and a condemning mind that isn't productive.

39. BATCH WORK DAYS

If you get in the habit of finding specific days to focus on same-type projects, you're more likely to complete or get deeper into that work and be more productive.

The quality of your work and what you do with the work improves.

If you teach, write, or present on the topic, you will be better prepared and more knowledgeable.

The secret to keeping good ideas is to keep a notepad handy so you can jot down ideas that come to you on the days you're not working on the project. This works well for lists where as soon as you put the list down, you'll come up with another idea.

If you're having trouble completing a project, find ways to be held accountable. Use a deadline, an accountability group, or partner to keep you from procrastinating and help you figure out what is slowing you down.

Use a habit of working 10 minutes a day or several uninterrupted hours one day a week to complete a project.

Little by little your large project is broken into sizeable chunks. It's easy to get in a rut when you work from home and you stare at a computer screen. Play music or spice up your experience with a decadent tea or spriter water in hand.

Every time you take a sip gives you a chance to take a split-second break that can get you back on course.

In Aesop's Fable, the tortoise finishes and wins because he's slow and steady, and moves along while the hare has the quick ability, but decides to take a nap.

Think of a time in your past when you didn't feel like doing something and you pushed through anyway and that resulted in the desired outcome.

40. ALLOW SPACE FOR YOU TO GROW INTO

Discover what work is most satisfying to you, and find a way to build into your day so you feel daily fulfillment. You can do this by simply changing your scenery. Take a walk or drive outside.

You can find muse breaks, and A-ha moments that you can easily miss if you're busy. Find a quiet place for you to get reflective even if it's just for a few minutes. See if anything comes up.

Often you get nothing back as you're inviting thoughts to come in. You're just warming up and revving up the engines for the day.

Then if you go back to doing an activity, then you can get the insight when least expected.

This is different if you book every minute of your day, where your life and calendar can be controlling you. Booking in breathing space is part of your wellness that catches up with any of us.

You are meant to grow and transform. Your identities can change as new defining moments enter.

If you decide you're happy with what you are or the "old you," consider you could be missing out if you're not sure about who you are. And you can explore if you get headspace.

You may discover that a sabbatical may be a good next step for this. They are not common as the concept isn't widely adopted but are becoming more popular. People are taking time to smell the roses while they have the most vitality.

A vacation extended is how a sabbatical can start. What you discover about yourself can be so revealing that you can't go back to the old ways or job if one is still there when your sabbatical ends.

You may find that what you thought you wanted in life isn't what you have. You can't go back in time, as a butterfly can't go back into its old cocoon or caterpillar life.

41. HIRE HELP FOR TASKS YOU DON'T ENJOY OR WHERE IT MAKES SENSE

When you don't enjoy activities, you're usually not as good with them as the ones you enjoy, as you don't apply all of you to the task.

At different times of your life, time vs. money vs. energy will be important. When you're younger, often it's money as there's not enough. Then when you're older, time is more valuable. You can want the work-life balance over the highest pay.

And when you're even older, energy is what you can most desire.

A smart move could be to hire help. Every little bit helps as your time is freed up. But what's most gained is the weight off your shoulders for emotional energy towards a task you don't enjoy.

If you're trying to get a business off the ground, if you keep your day job then you have the income to outsource cheaper labor tasks to others to do what you can't do while you're still working for an employer.

Tasks not only include ones you don't enjoy or don't have time to do, but also ones that you don't know what to do.

You don't have the expertise so you outsource and you learn better ways. It's almost like collaboration except the hired help works for you so you don't have to decide whose decision rules. Yours does.

42. RESET TO LOVING THOUGHTS AND FIND LOVE IN LIFE'S BEAUTY

Seek beauty in the everyday nature display, the greatest phenomenon we have as proof that there is a divine order to this life.

Find something larger than you to marvel at where you can stay in awe. That can be a man-made structure or art. If you go to the beach, you can find ornate sand sculptures that don't blow away and seem as though they have been there for years.

There's a mystery in who created the piece or was it more than one person? Wondering keeps us appreciating. That's what Stonehenge is all about.

To stay in balance, gather those moments recently where you felt gratitude and peace. Remind yourself of all the blessings you have. If you harbor resentment or feel bad, turn around your situation.

How can that same situation be worse? Then you can feel grateful.

When you develop less wanting as a new standard of love, then you can stop negative thoughts from trying to steal your day.

You have a compass that points north every time and doesn't spin around leaving you confused.

43. FIND TIME TO DREAM ABOUT THIS LIFE

If you feel like you're on a hamster wheel, getting time to be curious and question the obvious in this life can change your life in more ways than you can imagine now.

Somehow we stop dreaming as adults in our busyness and responsible roles. Discover about another culture, ocean life, or our ancestors.

Curiosity can breed innovation and new ways. We have new reasons to want to explore more of what this life is about.

That's the main mission of most museums to gain awareness and provide information.

44. LAUGH AND HAVE FUN

Laughter is a good medicine prescription. Being too serious and not taking time to smell the roses is life-depleting.

Growing up, we watched sitcoms that had the background audience laughing sounds. Laughter was a part of life and value for some people. There was less competition.

There were late-night comedy and variety shows. All that has been replaced with more serious genres and reality show competitions. Today's comedy is less wholesome, but in some ways more authentic.

Comedy in the past could be sarcastic. A woman could ask a man, "did you open the door for me because I'm a woman?" And the man could reply, "No, I opened the door because I'm a gentleman." These days a woman wouldn't commonly ask a daring question like that in our diversely sensitive world.

But you can find comic relief around if you look. You can watch the same entertainment over and over again and still belly laugh.

Find ways to bring back fun and laughter in your life. Both can be therapeutic. When you forget about the time in activities that put a smile on your face, then you are doing mental-health exercises.

45. FIND LIKE-MINDED NETWORKS AND GROUPS TO INTERACT WITH.

Be okay that your groups and people you associate with can change and overlap. If you seek personal growth, you will find new and old friends who are headed in the same direction as you.

When you bring in new friendships and groups, you're not abandoning old friendships. You're learning how to blend new and old friendships into your current life and who you are becoming.

If you're in a different season or on different pages than those you've been friends with, don't write them off.

That's an indication that change is brewing, a natural part of life.

Friendships like any relationship and situations go through different seasons. People enter your life for reasons and seasons. Those who last, pass the test of a good friendship.

If the friendship is made to last, time or distance apart won't change those divides.

Good relationships have a balance of giving and take, otherwise it's a lopsided relationship. As with everything else good in this life, sometimes a healthy break can prevent taking for granted ways, and so you can appreciate what you have.

You get a sense of what people are made of during tough times, as they still stay in touch. They don't just show up during your or their good times.

46. STAY GROUNDED. WHEN YOU CAN STAY HUMBLE AND PEACE-FILLED, THEN YOU BE INCREDIBLY USEFUL TO OTHERS

If you become successful, keep your centered ways and normalizing routines intact, always seeking healthy thoughts.

Healthy self-confidence isn't bragging. When you speak about yourself and your achievements, if you keep the authentic answers, then you will never have to regret your ways.

Being rooted solidly is admirable. People notice your ways even if they say nothing. They want to know what you know and have that makes you different and attractive.

47. FLIP ANY NEGATIVE PERSPECTIVE AROUND

Turn your work and life situations around (such as when you receive lemons, make lemonade). There is a flip side to almost all perspectives. Instead of having a sour attitude, add sweetness. You don't need to add backup plans.

You can stick with the ones you dream and aspire to have. Then while you're in the process of getting there, see that as the needed time to get prepared for the best result that is sustainable.

With setbacks and losses which all of us have faced, you have a choice to be thankful that you developed resilience, patience, compassion and broke some of your bad habits. You wouldn't have developed these traits if you had the same set of circumstances, but you were forced to and they forced you into a better person.

You stopped complaining, wanting, and acting like a victim because you knew if you wanted to change your day, you had to be the change.

48. FIND A CREATIVE ACTIVITY THAT USES A SIDE OF YOUR BRAIN THAT YOU DON'T USE IN YOUR WORK OR DAILY

This will help you relax and recharge. You may need a reminder, as the brain loves to point you to your old habits or your phone that uses the least amount of thought-prompting.

You could learn a new language, song or culture. You could dabble in art, photography, a new exercise, or try cooking or baking a recipe you're inspired to try. You could decorate a desk or nook area, create a new Zoom video background or a new dining room centerpiece.

If you want to know how well you have learned something, then teach someone else. That's a productive and natural way to apply your new knowledge and skills. You may need time and space for the information to sink in and digest.

49. FIND A WAY TO SPREAD MORE LOVING-KINDNESS TO YOUR DAY

When you're happy, you can better overflow in kindness. When you get, give and if you don't get, still give. This goes back to the good karma days where you want to put positive energy into the Universe.

Giving can be as simple as a "thinking of you" sentiment or encouraging someone along. Thinking of others and how you can help comes from inside. And when you don't have, if you give you will find you get more.

You'll experience how you can serve to positively impact and help others. You can reach out to loved ones and friends that you haven't talked to in a while. You can send an old photograph, a loving memory, or just send a personal note.

50. MIND-BODY BALANCE

I've saved the best for last. If you can find mind-body balance, then you will be living in harmony and good health, both mental and physical health.

You know when the mind-body balance is not present because you will be dissatisfied in every sense of the word. Your body will feel off and you can have malaise and unexplainable symptoms.

Sometimes past trauma has not been dealt with and can show up as a delayed response. That's what happened to me. I didn't realize I carried thoughts of lack and insecurity until I could distance myself and get aware of the invisible. Getting work-life balance and space to evaluate my life from an aerial view started the internal transformation.

In all of us, managing thoughts that come up is how you change your life from where you are and mindfully get the balanced living you want.

You can decide instantly to end your non-self-serving thoughts cold turkey in mid-thought by simply walking away. You do this using an acceptable personal standard as a marker. You know when you're not in that place because you feel drained.

You can reset getting good influence from your uplifting resources such as friends, stories, mentors, or books.

If for example, you find yourself falling negative in your speech because that's natural to you, question if that's good or bad, and then you can reflect deeper. Be conscious of your thoughts and actions.

And if you decide you want to change your language, then you can notice each time you make the faux pas, and substitute your words that help influence your thoughts.

To find out about restoring balance and happiness in your life, visit https://healthyhappylifesecrets.com

OTHER HELPFUL RESOURCES

Well + Good - https://www.wellandgood.com/

The Power of Now (Eckart Tolle)

Deepak Chopra books - The Book of Secrets, Perfect Health

READ OTHER 50 THINGS TO KNOW BOOKS

[50 Things to Know About Coping With Stress: By A Mental Health Specialist by Kimberly L. Brownridge](#)

[50 Things to Know About Being a Zookeeper: Life of a Zookeeper by Stephanie Fowlie](#)

[50 Things to Know About Becoming a Doctor: The Journey from Medical School of the Medical Profession by Tong Liu MD](#)

[50 Things to Know About Knitting: Knit, Purl, Tricks & Shortcuts by Christina Fanelli](#)

50 Things to Know

Stay up to date with new releases on Amazon:
https://amzn.to/2VPNGr7

CZYKPublishing.com

50 Things to Know

We'd love to hear what you think about our content! Please leave your honest review of this book on Amazon and Goodreads. We appreciate your positive and constructive feedback. Thank you.

www.ingramcontent.com/pod-product-compliance
Lightning Source LLC
Chambersburg PA
CBHW070301220526
45465CB00004B/1701